I0533270

The Power of words thoughts

and actions

By

Debbie Shirindzi

(Poety Expression)

The Power of words thoughts and actions

The Power of words thoughts and actions

Published by
Blessed Thabang Mobosi
Nkomaneni Dan C House No: 0601
Postal Address: PO Box 3275
Tzaneen 0850 Limpopo
South Africa

Email: Blessed.btm@gmail.com
Telephone 072 875 6983
Cell:
061 953 9726 / 067 817 2911

ISBN: 978-0-6399345-7-0

The Power of words thoughts and actions

Table of Contents

The Power of words thoughts and actions

DEDICATION

This book is dedicated to my precious parents Winnie and David Shirindzi, Moral, Shallotte, Gavaza, Gracious, Pretty, Dave, Immaculate, Lulama, Vukosi, Shiluva, Shilaveko. I dedicate to my pastor Mr. Baloyi everyone who pray for me and each one who read this book

1

Author Debbie Shirindzi

Debbie Shirindzi was born in 20 February 1998 in South Africa at Rhulani village under greater Tzaneen municipality South Africa Limpopo Tzaneen (Dan). She is the last born of her parents. She is a poet and motivator. She believes her calling is to become a social worker. She says the person who inspires her is her mother. Who is also her role model. She enjoys giving advices and hopes to become one of the best singers with a purpose of blessing people's life with her melodious voice. She is the last born of five daughters. Currently studying at the University of Venda, doing social work. She has the passion to improve and solve the issues that people face. She is a singer, motivational speaker and a modeler. A young black lady who create opportunities for herself. She founded an organization by the name of, "Sororal fraternal" that improves the life of people in Dan and Nkowankowa society.

A New Day

A day of celebration
Forgiving and forgetting
Start a new life, a life of fairy
A new day with new rain
That washes our sin
Provision of peace of joy
A new direction
To live and be an example

A new heart
Does not hold grudges
A new mind
Does not support the negative

A new tongue
Does not curse not even to insult
It does not judge
It is a tongue that blesses
It is a new day
Enjoy by giving blessing and smiling

Beauty

What is beauty?
A girl 's beauty is not appearance
Not about putting make-ups
Not even about wearing hills

Your beauty girl is your virginity
That is mine as well
At the age of 19 still pure
My pride my virginity
My dignity

The other reason for my confident
I will lose my pride when I'm ready to.
Not even by pressures
I am a virgin with a plan, with a purpose
Being virgin on this age means self-discipline
I am so beautiful
Create your beauty.

Happy Girl

She was insulted
She was called by names
They teased her
She never holds grudges
She smiled as if nothing happened
She danced to rhythms she understood
A happy girl
She sings praise songs
As if tomorrow does not exist
Today matters
She has no time to hate
She has a time to love
So confident
So happy
Prettiest girls are the happiest girls

I Am a Woman

I am a woman
A woman who is been hurt
A woman who is been betrayed
A woman who is been under minded

A woman who is been misjudged
A woman who cried a river
A woman who walked though thorns without
shoes
A woman who walked naked
I am a woman
A woman who is not afraid to shine
A woman who is not afraid to raise her voice
A woman who is not afraid to fail and try
again
A woman who is not afraid to walk the talk
I am a woman

That woman is genuine
That woman is confidant
That woman is beautiful
That woman is a treasure
That woman is inside
That woman is me
I am proud to be a woman

Myself

I am a bee
That produces honey
Honeybee in human
I am a smile keeper

Peace maker
A solution
A motivator
One in a million

Reasonable young lady
Short tempered
A virgin with a plan
So passionate
An apple of Jesus's eye
Oh yes, I am honeybee

A Lady
A made of man 's rip
A helper of a man
A queen in full
She knows how to comfort

How to reduce pain
To calm Brocken heart

Oh yes, she is a lady
Who respects her body?
Who dress well?

Who values her pride her virginity
"Walking with her head high'
She is proud to have Jesus
As her Lord and savior
A lady so reasonable, so intellect

She never
Forget her principles
A made of man 's rip
Behind every man there's lady

A Virgin with A Plan

A plan to be an example
For plenty young ladies
To remain pure to remain virgin
Until she gets married

A plan to prove and make all
To believe that 'Tsonga' young ladies
Know the meaning of dignity
Her virginity her dignity

A spear to fight a battle of volubility
A present for her parents
A speech to remain in their tongue
I am the lady my virginity my value

Half of My Life

My love
'My every day's crush'
I chose you
You are so handsome

Your balance outfits
You're speechy
Your deep, strong voice
You are my pride

Loving what you have
Loving who you are
You're personality rocks
The prince of my heart
Wanting to spend
Half of my life with you
U attract me

I chose you as you chose me
The real king on the way

Fallen in Love

So in love
So bright both day and night
Your presence supplies joy to my soul
Peace of my heart

A bling of my eyes
A honey on my lips
Having you around is a blessing
I could always ask for
I am carried away by you
So insane in love with you
You showed love
I gave joy

Who Am I?
A young lady
A princess not for all
But for those who value her
A reasonable and understanding
Young lady

Who know how to sacrifice for her loved
ones?
I am a treasure in the eyes of my parents
The remover of pressure
A peace maker, who hate to be treated like a
troublemaker,

She is smart
So intelligent
She is a motivator
I am a princess

SISTERS

Tearing out tears of pain
Bleeding inside outside
You are lost
Stop aborting babies

Those babies are innocent
Stop killing their purpose to live
My dad in heaven
Created them in his image

Stop aborting his image
Stop abusing your rights
The bill of rights
A human has a right to live
A right of life

Who are you to commit a crime?
Who are you to break the laws?
The wages of sin is death
You commit crime you pay for it

If you ever become barren, you'll wish that
baby lived. Your wish will remain a wish
Forever caring guilt

I am tearing tears of blood
Stop aborting babies
For they are special being

Babies

So cute
So harmless
So precious
So prevailing
A new life

A new reason to live
Made of Jesus
A pride
A blessing

An angel
Filled with life
Filled with purpose
Babies are adorable
A life itself
A leader of tomorrow

Try and See

She gives people pluck
She speaks about life
From her point of view
Her words are comforting
Her words heal the wounded hearts

Wherever she goes
She carries the calabash of dignity on her
head
She talks less about her inner bleeding
People are blinked by her well fashioned eyes
They think that she has it all

The wound of her heart
Displays in her eyes
Her Brocken soul
Her intolerable pain
Hidden by the corners of her eyes
Sometimes she gets carried away
Only God knows her reason
For being mortal
She measures her life by the scale of a salt
Only her eyes can tell the truth.

Pain

Pain removes joy
Turn life to dearth
It removes peace
It supplies desperation

It supplies complication
Introduce illness
Pain! Pain! Pain!
A partner of sorrow

Death itself
Avoid pain
Pain is a weapon to dig grave
"Turn your harmful feelings into your
Healing emotions"
Pain removes joy

Peace

What a feeling
So, discipline
 So happy
So passionate in a positive way
A combination of life and Jesus
Living simple life

Enjoying who you are
So, exerting
So energetic
Stress free

Peace one can create themselves
Peace rules the kingdom
Peace is a feeling

Poverty

Poverty exists
I have seen it
I have heard about it
Some experienced it

Lazy to study, bunk classes
Rejecting positive advices
It does lead to poverty

Loving blanket and bed
As if it was created today
Forgetting we found it here
We will die and leave it here
Stop rejecting education

Stop rejecting knowledge
Stop fooling yourselves
Life with no education is a life to berg
Is an application to be nobody
A truck of poverty does exist

Forever followed with misery
Never apply for poverty
Is like bearing in hell
While living under the sun

Who I Am?

Who am I?
Where do I come from?
What am I doing here?
I am honeybee
Coming from poverty

I am here to fight poverty
I am honeybee
Produced by worker bees
A hard-working young lady
Who shines both in dark and light.
I am a solution
Peace maker
Smile keeper

An apple in the eyes of my love ones
You are an apple as well
We are both the answers
A wealth and joy in our family

Youth

Young adult
Fresh vegetables
Filled with life
Lot of goals to fulfill

Dreams to archive
So passionate
So energetic
Realize where you are from
Who you are?
Who do you want to be?

Support your dreams
Chase opportunities
Be confident to turn it into reality
You are so valuable
A perfect creation
Never limit your self

"The sky is the limit"
Accept positive advices
Listen to motivations
Life without planning
Is like planning to fail

Take Care

Take care of yourself
Your surrounding's
Care is part of love
Part of discipline
It begins deep inside
Deep in you

It exists in our soul, in our veins
Care is a personality
Love everything
Care for everything
"Charity begins at home"

It Is Normal

Fall in love
Be crazy in love
Craving of kisses
Feeling lonely
Without the one you love

It is normal
Jealousy overwhelmed
When your crush surrounded by different gender

It is normal
Feeling anger when your crush treats you like a stranger
It is normal but, though hurting
Not returned by love, when you love
It is normal

Shower them with love
Though they shower with hatred
It is normal
The nature of your surroundings
Is the way you are

Pointless

Oh yes, it is point less
Bonding with those who hate you
Invited on a party
Feeling alone in the middle of everyone

Treated like a stranger while you were
invited
Moment of selfies, but pushed away
They invited you
But forget you

So boring plenty of regretting
Heavy rain falls from my sexy eyes
Stop hurting yourself
By creating bond with those
Who know nothing about relationship?

Appreciate what you have
Accept people who love you
Stop hurting yourself

One Day Thing

Touching kissing it was the thing
Smiling taking pictures
It was part of a day
Bounding with friends

Being part of them
It was the best of it all
A day of joy

Unforgettable day
So, exerting so excited
Oh yes one day thing
A thing to remember
Part of good memories
One day thing

Never

Never laugh those in pain
You might not know
The cause of the pain
Never lough
Never point fingers to the disabled
You might end up perfectly like them
Never mistreat the poor

While you are wealthy
You might not know
What might happen tomorrow?
Never hurt others you will suffer
The consequences
"Walk with the wise you will become wise
If you walk with fools, you will suffer the
harm"

Today is me, tomorrow is you

Slaves of Our Own

Our brothers and sisters died yesterday
Just for you and me to have freedom today
They raised their voices higher yesterday
For you and me to be heard today

In the cold night they slept on their roof,
yesterday
For you and me to sleep in our well-built
houses today

They fought for our right yesterday
For us to use them today
We fail to practice safe sex today
For our children to be safe tomorrow
We fail to see condom as our protector today

For our children to see him as their savior
tomorrow
We fail to see aids as the devil today
For our children to worship condom
tomorrow
Aid's is free and we are doomed.

Betrayed by Friends

She fooled me by her silly ways
She united me and him
As if she is a saint
She turned me into a crack
So close to the guy

She seduced him
She is a slut
He was attracted to her
They both united like a game
So, blinded by their smiles

Missing the guy
My friend the guys playing hide and seek
He left her she was alone
She lost my trust and now has her space
She was forever alone since she was self-centered
Slowly dying alone
"A trator pays with tears"

Stranger

I remember it, like it was yesterday
The first day you cared
Your hands were very gentle
The warmth of your arms
Like wings you wrapped me

The softness of your lips
Your lips were soft and sweet
You were speaking words of life
You used to embrace me

But now you have changed
The old you is forever gone
Like a stranger you touched me
As somebody who is passing by, you talk to
me
Your love now feels like......

You are in my skin against my will
You have become darkness in my life
I remember it, like it was yesterday.

Broken Heart

Felt in love with so called a guy
Who knew nothing about love
A liar a deceiver
Who never sticks to his words
So disgracing
So disappointing

Who easily play with emotions
Easily to misuse time
Who became a curse
Not a blessing in a girl 's life
Venom with unbreakable pain
A pain to kill not to hurt

He thought to be smart, a fool instead
To collect broken pieces, it was a duty
Accept what cannot be changed
Heal adopt peace
You chose what is happening in your life
So, take control

Brake Up

In relationship
Everything flows like river
So sweet like honey
Both deeply in love
Just as deep as ocean

Overcoming difficulties together
Climbing all negatives
Flow all positive
Just like the mountain

Celebrating anniversaries of born days
So happy
 So proud

Overnight everything fades away
As if nothing happened
As if you both have no past together
You broke up

Treating each other like strangers
Let it, move on
It is done, it is brake up
It happens to lot so do not stress

December Time

A busy month
So funny and sunny
We smile and smite
Like angels in fairy tale
We love each other

We are the peace makers
Smile keepers
Love expresser
God loves me and
I love him

Jehovah

The creator of heaven and earth
The provider of safety day and night
He gives life
He gave me a chance to repent
He is a parent of the orphan's
He gives courage

Strength to overcome all
He rescued me from darkness to light
From sickness to healthy
From death to life
Dad you deserved to be worship
You are holy...

Jesus Heals

Oh yes, he does
He is our healer
The one who comforts us
Plenty lost their husband
Lost their kids
He healed them

They are moving on
Some lost their parents
They lost their siblings
Lost their business
They were divorced

Some failed
Jesus healed them
Accept him to be part of you
He will heal all kinds your of pains
Bring you joy
Life in full
Jesus the son Jehovah.

Jesus

Jesus my dad's son
The creator 's son
Who died for you and me
His dad is my creator
The creator of heaven and earth
The most high and powerful God

The father of nations
The king of kings
The Lord of lords
Who was who is to come
Who knew you and I
Before the world did

Who created us with a purpose
Our life giver
Our protector
Our healer
Our advisor
He forgives our sins
Our provider
Jesus love you, so do I

Benefit

Hey there
Love me or hate me
I benefit nothing out of it

My success, my safety depends on Jesus
No one can take my life nor my gift
Only God can, for he is the creator
I am an apple of my father's eye

The treasure the remover of pressure
Never force to be loved
Never cry, if they hate you
A human's hatred a human 's love
Does not feed you no to count your life
Hey there listen
"The best part about learning is that
No one is going to take it away from you"

Real Beasties

Besties respect emotions
Never hurt intentionally
Never break heart
They know the meaning of relationship
They are harmless
Not fragile, but strong

They support, and they stick to each other.
Even when one is wrong
To show another the right path
They know how to sacrifice
How to protect

How to keep each other happy
Real Besties have each other's back
At all times
Besties love each other

Overnight

I was your girl
Until you define me your ex
So hurting, so disappointing
I was proud to have you
Overnight felt insulted
To be called your ex

The day I met you I was cursed
Cursed the word, "yes" that combined you
and me. Your apologies are so light
I love you from your lips felt empty
You disgust me

Trapping me the whole night
Meanwhile we did nothing
Overnight you opened my eyes
I felt the bond of my real people
How they are attached to me

How I missed them my family
Overnight I stopped liking you
You turn out to be a stranger
Everything blown by wind
It happened over night

The Lost Generation

The generation without knowledge of the past
They know nothing about their ancestors
They know nothing about tradition
"Each and everything that is happening in our life
It began right in our mind

We are the generation with no dreams to archive
No goals to fulfill
We have no motive of our own
No courage to change our country
Not even yourself

People win and fail in their mind
We talked back to our teachers at school
Our parents at home
The elders along the way
Young ladies we are turning ourselves into whores
We are involved with married men
Forgetting we are taking away our pride our value

Young men you are brutally killing people

Forgetting they are human they have feelings
You have no conscious
No sympathy
Oh yes, we are the lost generation
Is that really what we are?
Is that really what we choose to be?

Tears of Joy

Tearing out
Day and night
That brightens my way
God gave me a gift
So exerted,

So confident
Filled with peace
The heart that Forgives unconditionally
A soul overwhelmed with joy
So strong, so bold
The sun rose
The life seems fair
What a feeling
"Ntsako na ku nandziya (Joy with sweetness)
Wa ti endlela (You create unto yourself).

You Call It Love

Wanting myself to text you
At all times while we are both online
But you call it love
You spend more time with your friends less
with me.
More attention to your friends

Less to myself
But you call it love
You cheat I found out
You dump and cheat again
Calling me your wife
Who is your desert?
Who is your side chic?

An yet you call it love
You slap me every now and then
As a result of your wrong deeds
You do more wrongs
Still you call it love

Do not be fooled that is not love
Forever remember love is joy
Love never hurts! Loving wrong ones
Is what hurts.

The Guy

I met a guy
Who knows the meaning?
Of a relationship
So handsome
 So wise

He is filled with joy
So confident and brave
He is handsome and strong
My smile keeper

Love giver
He motivates me
With how love life is
He gives tips and tricks of life success
To live simple love life
He is a real friend
My treasure
My remover of pressure

Dad

Awesome daddy
So loving, so caring
An example of a man
The head of my family
Who appreciate what he has

Who treat mom like a queen
 Treating his kids like the prince and princess
You gave your family a name
You gave fairly life
Is a blessing to have you
You are special
So grate
Happy father's day

My Africa

How exclusive you are
Alone I lie on my back
Next to your stream
Making it beautiful sound
That no man can do

The grass is freshly green
In perfect size for me
To wave my hand on
Birds singing very softly
To accompany my loneliness

The sky is so blue and cloudy
Are in perfect semblance
The sun's rays are fine
Many kinds of flowers
So glare and glimmering
Allowing me to slowly tear them
Forever I will cherish you

My Father

The head of my family
An example of human
Who know the meaning of unity

The meaning of bringing joy to his family
The one who accept responsibility
The one who shape kids
And cultivate his belongings
A parent who practice fairy tale on the house
The one who is willing to protect
A father
A hero
A king
My role model

Songs

Songs heal Brocken souls
Broken hearts
They remove stress and remove stressors
They terminate the kingdom of loneliness
And place it with the kingdom of entertainment
Songs motivate those with no courage
They give strength to those who lost hope
They remove unsurity of you
They place in confidence
They place self-discovery

Songs control anger
Songs create new soul
On the old body
Love songs
Avoid getting hurt
Songs tell stories

Lost Joy

She lost her joy
She lost her husband
She lost it all
After trying to have kids
Craving for noise

Wishing to be called mommy
Pleading another reason to live
It was all she can wish for
She aborted two innocent kids
She took their right to live
Her wrong deeds are wiping her
She's forever without a baby

Forever lost her joy
She was divorced, she took her life
"A result of sin
Is dearth"
She lost her joy
She lost her life

Green Tea

Medicine for plenty diseases
Preventation of plenty stressors
Limitation of some worries
Turning obese body into skinny ones
Medicine of activeness
A path to be healthy
"Green tea"
 One of the best teas

Obsession

I am insane
Desperately in love
The love I call it mine,
While the owners are there
Jealous take the best of me
Ladies around him
He enjoys them
 I am drying inside
So scared to lose him, but already lost him
I mistook obsession for love
Hatred and anger lead me
Obsession disrupts
Desperation controls

It's all reward regrets'
Let go of what it cannot be changed
Forgive yourself heal and have peace b
Be happy have courage be confident
That is part of life

"It is all fair in love, war and debate"
It is fair on friendship

Hurt

Loving you seemed to be a blessing
But a curse instead,
Having you around seemed to be an
opportunity
But an insult it became
You did hurt my feelings
Shunted my hopes

My wishes disappeared
You pushed me away
Like a stranger
You consider me weak
Measurable young lady
I used to consider you strong
Valuable young men
What a pity

It is part of my past
Never let go of your confidence
Reason being pain, makes you strong
Let go of those who hurt you
Enjoy what you have yourself

Love

Love is joy
Love never hurt
Misunderstanding does
Love is care not pity

Love led to life not death
Love has no condition
No attention no love
No love no care
No care no life

Love is respect, not fear
Love is willing not force
Love does not hurt
Loving the wrong person does
Love and joy do not separate
"Love your neighbor the way you love
yourself"

It Is Love

"A very strong liking"
A combination of care and attention
Value of joy towards each other
Visibility of real smile real hugs
Hugs with no betrayal
 Kiss without pretending

Smile with no fooling
Exchange of love towards each other
Love a golden feeling
An apple of bright eyes

Rose planted in the garden of love
So passionate
Love defeat hatred
Love has no condition
"Love a very strong liking"

Sweetheart

Loving you that much
Smelling your perfume from distance
Feeling your presence, from miles away
Your looks do me good
Loving you unconditionally

The joy you, give overflow
The kiss glows
I am your princess
You are my prince
Together we rule the kingdom
Full of happiness of love
Sweetheart you are the best
"Loving each other it was never a crime"

Love back

I loved you
We were items
We broke up
It was a deep of my childishness
Asking love back was the only thing can be done

You laughed at me
I was broken
I gave up
You return for love?
No longer interested
You thought it was a prank(joke), but no it was not

I moved on from that moment
"He mistook gold for a stone"
His loss
So happy with my new guy
You are sad and forever am gone
Never misuse the chance
When love back is asked
Be yourself enjoy life
When you get a chance

Men

The sixth creation as a human
On the earth surrounded by animals
So brave
Knowing how to handle a pain
How to hide tears
So responsible

Accepting responsibilities as amen
So passionate about his world
He knows how to love her
Know how to treat his lady as a queen

A gentleman he is
Who knows seasons and how to react on
those?
Who does not take advantage of those
without knowledge?
A man who does not abuse his right

A Cover Friend

So close we were
Similar cloth we wore
Same plays we watched
Same dance we loved
I used to love you
So much as a sister

Time and again
Bad thing you did
My name on mud
Of your family you placed
Solo after another
Of your folks knew I was
For we were close
Distanced to be in mono-world
You lied to be good
In all eyes who knew us
Friendship fades away
With different intentions
Same world we walked
Opposite purpose we had
A friend under self-interest you were
Pathways we did
So close we were
Not anymore

True Friend

Take a book and study
While others rush to fun
Take shower to church
While others rush to pub
Remember the real you
In downswings in upswing of life

Path of prosperity provides
Empower in all you do
She got your back
True friends hard to get
Take books and study
Only the true friend does
Solution and joy, they are.

Path of prosperity they lead you to

A Friend Have My Man

Self-interest comes first
Everything I archived
Everything I have
So powerful it is
So priceless it is

Friend have my man
His number you stole
You called and seduced him
All issues we had you fixed
A loving friend role you played

He was life to me you knew
I loved him you knew
A poison to disperse Us you became
He was supposed to marry me
You replaced got married instead
A friend on my man
Lesson I learned not to trust
Everything I had
You always want
Self-interest comes first
In all friendship
Never trust a friend
Friend have my man

Friend to My In-Law

Two and half years
Friends we have always been
Never in competition
Never betrayed one another
Never we caused another sorrow
Always, I valued you
A twin I saw Friend
Friend to my in-law
A flower my brother saw in you
Married you were
Traditionally along with legality
Sister in-law from friend
On my parents you
Tried to replace me
You tried to turn
My own brother against me
On my relatives you
Tried to replace me
Selfish you turned to be
Day after another you tried
To snatch my happiness
To sister in-law from friend
Angel you used to be
Devil himself you are
Friend to my in-law

Friend with a friend

I met you, valued you
I cared, I loved you
More than a friend I had
Forgotten her love
Forgotten all the best
She brought in me
Moment after another
I pushed her, I hurt her

She never complained
You betrayed her
Stole her shares
On the company we built
I let you as you mattered

Million pieces she breaks down
Again, I chose you over her
Today you slept, you are married
To my man my love
You slot my back
She always gave
You always took
Her value today I see
An angel she is she was
A friend with a friend

Friend Between My Parents

Mom and dad always
Always loved you
Like their own baby
After your late mom
Mom became your mom
Dad took responsibility of you
My house was our home
Mom clothed you, fed you
She gave all she can

A friend between my parents
My dad you seduced
The husband of the lady
That gave you new identity
You slept with
So ashamed I felt of you
I threw you out

I hated you
my parents recovered
Strong than before
In the street you sleep, you eat
Opportunity mom gave
On mud you placed
Friend between my parents

Friend on My Ex

To the core of my heart
On my inner circle I placed you
A friend I saw
A friend I felt I have
A traitor you prove to be

In four days, my love
Turned into my ex
So, connected we were
So, in love we were
You met you talked
You knew him, and how I love him
You replaced me

A saint you pretend to be
Apology you asked
I forgave you to have peace
With myself to move on
Friendship you asked
On my territory

A friend I saw
A stranger I see
Friends cannot be trusted

On the Graveyard He Was Placed

Part of grave he was, as he died
On top of his grave, he set
Surrounded by uncountable
Dreams needed to be archived.

Wishing to be fulfilled
Questioning his fate
His way of doing things
A singer he was supposed to be
A loud maker he was in his room

A poet he was
His work was never read
Best dancer he was
Never enjoyed the benefit of it
Smart he was
But did nothing to represent himself

Time waits for no man
Every single day passed
He did nothing when he had chance

Never be like him
Do all work in all seasons
To up stain I should have

On top of his grave he set
With his dreams questioning his fate
Change your pace of doing things

Identify Real Friend

A beautiful young girl
From fortunate family
A lot hated her, for her personality
A friend she met
A friend who loved her
A friend who valued her
A friend who has her back
As she was popular
She kept meeting new people
People who want what she has
People who want to destroy her
Time waits for no men
She lost track to see
Track to identify real friend
She chose a traitor
Over a real friend
A traitor stole her man

Settled down with him
Her old friend she searched
A real friend she identified
Forever they were friends
Stood by each other
All they overcome
Forever they were happy

Loving one another
By the name of friendship

A Thought to Have Any Men

A side chick in all relationship you are
For you never see it as big deal
Beautiful body you have
A thought to have any men
You always say your motto it is
To tear apart families
To separate young couples
You did it as you're proud
Your friend 's ex
Is your boyfriend
You live and think no more
For tomorrow

All the sons and their fathers know you
More than the way you know yourself
Advices to you is waste of strength
Today hospital bed is part of you
Your life is tarnished, so young you are
A thought to have any men
Your motto it was
You teared families apart
You separated young couples
You lived and think no for tomorrow.

She Have Your Man

As a friend she always saw you
A slut you were, not planning to change
She never introduced you
To the one she calls her love
On Facebook you searched him
Loose trouser he was
You searched him you found him
You slept to the bed your friend was
A disgrace of friend you are
You teared her apart she let him go

She has your man
Love and joy define them
Settled down they are
He let you go, red meat you are
Value you lost a friend you lost
A love partner you lost
You searched her man
You kept him for you

She has your man
Settled happily married they are
You searched him loneliness you got

Build What You Want

Details after another you knew
She shared all her thought
All her joy with you
So happy in relationship she was
Details after another she told you
For her, you were never happy
Always you were in love
With her handsome king
She never saw it

You never mentioned it
Time and again you planned
To take her life
Fate never in your side
Build what you want
Stop placing yourself

Where you have no place
She shared all with you
You're now taking all from her
Jealous never pays, so to opposition
Build what you want
Stop placing yourself
Where you have no space

Twins You Are Them

From childhood always you were friends
Same color same design cloth you wore
Twins you like them
You got each other 's back
You protected one another
Friends that really love one another you were
All girls wished to be like you
Birth day's celebration after another you did
Sisters you saw in one another
Same men you fall in love with
The lucky one has him
The other let go
Friendship like this one
Never have I ever saw
Shining stars, you were
In the middle of ordinary ones
From childhood always you were friends
Twins you are

Build Your Own Man

Build what you want
Clean your own road
A man to take your hand on stares
A man to paint your nails
A man to comb your air

A man to hold umbrella for you
A man to cook for you
A man to feed you
A man to respect you
A man to love you
A man to treat you like Queen
You build him

Any man can be that man
Man need to be thought
How to do things
Man need to be told
What we want in relationship
Man are treated with respect
Make him feel loved
Make him feel blessed to have you
Build what you want
Clean your own road

Build Your Own Lady

Ladies are like babies
They need attention
They need to feel loved
They must be respected
They must be spoiled

They must be asked what they love
What makes them happy?
Ladies are not punching begs
Ladies are not machine to make babies
Ladies are treasures

They're remover of pressure
Build your own lady
Any lady can be cultivated to what you want
Turn her to hot sexy lady
Dress her more than slay Queens
A prostitute can be that lady
Church girl can be that lady
Loose skirt can be that lady
Build your own lady

One in A Million

My king I call you for the love I feel for you
For the respect I have for you
For the position you have in my life
So fortunate to have you I feel
You feel my heart with joy
You feel my mind with fairy tale
You feel my soul with peace
So much I love you

One in the million to be called king
One in the million to be spoiled
One in the million to be respected
One in the million to be loved
You are the best of them all
My king you are

My king I call you for the love I feel for you
For the respect I have for you
For the position you have in my life
So fortunate to have you I feel
So much I love you

Amazing Women

Amazing woman my mom is
Winnie she was named
So kind she is.

A heart of an angel she has
She gives without counting
Her cloth, she feed both
Her own blood and not
She feeds with love
She cloth us the word of God
She teaches humanity

A definition of a mother
Perfectly defines her deeds
Lot betrayed her, plenty hurt her
She forgives and blesses all
Mom your way of loving is amazing
Your presence means life

You give me courage
From the core of my heart
From a thin layer of my soul
I adore I appreciate who you are
You are my galaxy

The amazing woman I never met
You are my priceless gift
My treasure my life
Amazing woman my mom is

Woman Defines Love

A woman that defines love
You are a witness as I am
Your love amazes me
Woman like yourself
To meet in this life blessing it is

You have your own kids
Still you loved me like your own
A doll of four headed you gave me
I appreciate it a big role it played
For myself to choose a person I want to be
Yellow jacket you gave me
To keep me warm
From 14 of age today 22 of age
I still wear it, fit me as well
School Jessie you bought me
Your love amazes me
A lot you did for my family
We all appreciate it

Never will we forget you
Amazing woman you are
A mother of all you are
Humanity defines you
Amazing woman you are

Best Father

A man who think more for his kids
Thankless of himself
You were you and will always be
The best father, great man
Traditions call your name
To kneel before greeting elders
From childhood to lady hood
You taught I

Your upbringing means life
To offer guest a sit, food
Always you emphasized
Humanity defines your kindness
David that's your name
Dad you are the best

You fed us, you clothed us
Good accent of English you taught
Knowledge you impacted in me
The word, "father" defines you
To pass my grade contribution you were
Assignment homework after another
You helped me to write

School meetings, always available

Success prosperity, always wanted for me
Dad so much I love you
I appreciate you for who you are
You are my life my purpose
The best father among fathers

The Power of Arts

Expression of emotion art it is
He lost the one he calls family
To understand his pain
No one did he felt loss

Paintings drawings defined
His loss, his pain
Art heal unknown wounds
Expression of illusions art it is
Lot called her insane
For she speaks thing
No one never thought of

Drawings painting turns illusion
Into a beautiful art
 All want to keep
Art color grey world

Art is amazing work
A lot ask where people
Sow what they draw
Illusions emotions make it
Possible to draw things from another planet
The power of art color the world

What Is Love

Love is good attention
One give to someone
Love is caring for that one
Feels for the next person
Love is happiness

One brings in your life
Love is appreciating
All the deeds our loved ones commit

Do in our life to keep us happy
Love is listening
Without interruption
Love is advising without
Blaming anyone

Love is to accept one
Without putting price of conditions
Love is beautiful
Love combine everything
What is love?

Jesus In My Life

Miracle after another he did
In the middle of the darkness
Death was the only thing felt
To see the following day
Hope I lost, I gave up already
Jesus my protector

 A life you gave me
Light you gave, darkness fade
Strength you gave, strong I felt
He never gave up on me
He never failed me

Always as he said he is here
I sow his deeds
Jesus is alive
Jesus in my life
Miracle after another he did

Father God

With your image I was created
So, chosen I feel I am
So stunning I am
A gold has no value in me
So precious I am

A solution to questions I am
Confidence you gave me
For you are not shy yourself
I call myself your child
Forever I will reap the seed I sow
Father God for life
I highly appreciate it
With your image I was created